Home Field Advantage

by

Gary H. Goldberg

ISBN: 1-4184-1882-X (e-book)
ISBN: 1-4184-1883-8 (Paperback)

Library of Congress Number: 2004091883

Printed in the United States of America
Bloomington, IN

This book is printed on acid free paper.

First published by AuthorHouse 04/06/04

I dedicate this book to my Dad, who could beat any team of aliens with one hand tied behind his back.

CHAPTER ONE

July 9, 2000

4:15 p.m.

Joni relaxed on the lounge chair behind her home overlooking Crestview Park. She was 15 years old, five feet, five inches tall, 130 pounds and considered, by most, to be one of the best pitchers, male or female, in Massachusetts. Her dad had begun teaching Joni the game when she was only two, old enough to carry a plastic baseball bat and strong enough to hit a Wiffle ball. Joni had a mean "slurve" and a dead-eye fast ball. She was quick on the base paths and could hit well to all fields. She also understood the mystique of the game itself. Joni truly loved baseball and all that it represented: its traditions, history, the connection to family, home team loyalty and the sense of pride Americans had for their national past time.

*****

Crestview Park had two baseball fields, a small one for the younger kids, called Yaz Field, and a major league size

1

baseball field called Jackson Field, for those with dreams of playing in the "bigs." Joni had played on Jackson since she was seven. For years, she came out early in the morning before school and practiced pitching with her dad. After dinner, they walked the field, discovering every hole, rough, hill, angle, blind spot and shadow, which could give them an advantage and their opponents a nightmare. They created nicknames and signals for the "elite eight."

PITCHER'S MOUND, aka "rabbit's foot" (adjust pants). The hole in front of the pitcher's mound was shaped like a rabbit's foot, causing pitchers with large, wide feet to lose their balance in delivering the ball to home plate.

BATTER'S BOX, aka "the coffin" (fist to chest). The batter's box was comprised of very loose dirt around home plate, causing runners to sink in and get a very slow start to first base.

THIRD BASE, aka "the grave" (hat off head). The third base area was very rocky and hard, resulting in balls taking crazy hops.

THIRD BASE LINE, aka "the sand box" (wipe feet). A bunt between home and third that hugged the third base line would be stranded in quicksand – the ball would simply die there.

LEFT FIELD LINE, aka "the slide" (hand across the letters). In left field, grass did not grow. As a result, the ball bounced extremely hard and the player's spikes slid on the fast surface.

<u>LEFT CENTER,</u> aka "the ditch" (hand behind knees). Due to the age of the field, there was a drainage ditch in left center. Several players caught their spikes in the ditch, causing severe sprains, broken ankles and torn ligaments.

<u>RIGHT CENTER FIELD,</u> aka "the cat's tail" (pat head). In right center, there was a narrow ditch that had the shape of a cat's tail. It was similar to a small grand canyon. The balls would hit the tail, bouncing in all directions.

<u>RIGHT FIELD LINE,</u> aka "hornets' nest" (pat face). Hornets built a nest in a small hole in the ground. Running too close to the nest increased the likelihood of being stung, resulting in a missed fly ball or an extra base hit.

As she sat back in her lounge chair, Joni smiled. She never lost on her field. She could not wait for her next game. Joni did not realize, however, that her next game could very well be her last.

CHAPTER TWO

July 9, 2000
4:30 p.m.

As Joni was about to doze off, a news flash came over the radio: "Aliens have landed on Earth... Aliens have landed on Earth!"

In Atlanta, a space ship from Mars landed in Olympic Stadium. The game between the Braves and the Pirates came to an immediate halt. Twelve Martians emerged from the small shuttle- craft wearing red and black baseball caps and matching uniforms. The word *'MARTIANS'* was written in black script across their red uniforms. A red sphere with a black bat appeared as a logo on their hats. The Martians were between six and seven feet tall with two very long arms and two human-size legs. Their hands were very large, with three long fingers and a thumb. Their feet were small, but very wide. Their faces were round and purplish. Their eyes were extremely large, located on the sides of their heads. Their noses were inverted with three small holes for nostrils. There was no visible hair on their head or face: no beards, eyelashes or eyebrows. Their teeth were brown, apparently from chewing tobacco. Their ears began next to their eyes and continued in a crisscrossed pattern over the top of their heads. In fact, the Martians' heads resembled purple baseballs.

It was clear that these aliens came to play baseball. No weapons, no threats, JUST baseball. A press conference was scheduled for 7:00 p.m.

CHAPTER THREE

July 9, 2000

7:00 p.m.

The press conference was held at the southern office of the Baseball Commissioner. The Martians' manager took center stage. The rest of his team stood behind him. All of Earth watched and waited on his every word.

"Citizens of Earth. My name is Casey. I, along with my team, are here on behalf of our home planet Mars. Martians truly enjoy playing baseball. Our world has been watching your planet for 100 years, studying and learning about this game America calls its national pastime. We have adopted baseball as our global sport. We have dedicated our very existence to becoming the galaxy's best baseball players. We are here to put true meaning to your World Series."

"Let me introduce our players. They are the best our world has to offer:

First Base	Lou
Second Base	Honus
Shortstop	Ozzie
Third Base	Mike
Left Field	Ted
Right Field	Babe
Center Field	Joe
Catcher	Yogi
Pitcher	Sandy
Pitcher	Bob
Relief Pitcher	Goose"

The players stepped forward as their names were called, tipped their hats to the television audience and then immediately stepped back in line. All of their movements were in perfect harmony.

"As you can see, we have come to love and admire the heroes of your game. We have come to Earth to play baseball. We propose a three game series. On Mars, we have adopted the rules played by the National League of the United States of America. We do not believe in the designated hitter. We also do not believe in pinch runners or pinch hitters. Our players bat both righty and lefty, and our pitchers pitch with either hand. We will allow you, however, to play with as many players you choose and to substitute as freely as you wish. You may even have more than nine players on the field at any time. If you win just one game, we will consider ourselves to have lost and will return immediately to our planet. If we win, you must agree never to play baseball again. If you do not accept our challenge, we will assume that your players do not have the ability or the courage to play against the best. We will wait until 1:00 p.m. tomorrow for your answer."

CHAPTER FOUR

July 9, 2000

9:00 p.m.

Fred Johnson was the Baseball Commissioner. He had assumed the position in 1998 after a five year vacancy. After a brief upswing in baseball's popularity during the historic "Yankee Year" of 1998, baseball in the year 2000 was once again in turmoil. The leagues had grown further apart. The players' and umpires' unions were getting stronger and more vocal. Players' salaries were "out of this world." Attendance was down. More school-age children were playing soccer and football than baseball. Major League Baseball had not yet expanded into Europe like the National Basketball Association. Discipline of high priced players was a joke. And now the Martians wanted to play ball! The Commissioner was truly facing a major dilemma. If we lose, no more baseball. If we elect not to play, we will be the laughingstock of the galaxy. And if we do play, which players get selected? What stadium? Which umpires? What time of day? And, if that were not enough, an answer was needed by 1:00 p.m. tomorrow!

CHAPTER FIVE

July 9, 2000

Sunday Night

The phones never stopped ringing in the Commissioner's office that night. Presidents past and present, team owners, politicians, Hall of Famers, the press, corporate America, advertisers, celebrities, drunks, school children, homemakers – all called with an opinion. The consensus was to play the games, the first at Yankee Stadium in New York on Tuesday night (July 11), the second, if necessary, at Dodgers' Stadium in Los Angeles on Friday afternoon (July 14), and the third game was left open, but to be played that Sunday (July 16). The excitement and fear generated by the Martians was so enormous that all non-essential businesses and schools came to a halt until the games were played. No one could decide whether the Martians were to be trusted.

As for the players, the first game was going to be played by a team of All-Stars from the National and American Leagues. If a second game was needed, players from other countries would be considered. As for the third game, no decision was made. It made everyone too nervous to think about playing one final game for the right to play baseball for all eternity. By Sunday, baseball could be a thing of the past.

CHAPTER SIX

Tuesday, July 11, 2000

THE NEW YORK NEWS

GAME 1 OF THE WORLD SERIES TO START TONIGHT. PLAYERS SELECTED. WORLD WAITS IN ANTICIPATION.

The Baseball Commissioner formally accepted the Martians' proposal to play a series of three baseball games, beginning tonight at Yankee Stadium. Bobby Cox was named Manager of the All-Star team, with Joe Torre as his third base coach and Tommy Lasorda as his first base coach. Twenty-five players were selected for the team by Cox and his coaching staff. Nine pitchers and 16 everyday players were chosen based upon their statistics over the past two years. Cox made the team selections known yesterday at 12:00 noon.

	Starting Lineup	Reserves
1B	Frank Thomas	Mark McGwire
2B	Carlos Baerga	Roberto Alomar
3B	Chipper Jones	Vinny Castilla
SS	Alex Rodriguez	Derek Jeter
LF	Tony Gwynn	Barry Bonds
RF	Juan Gonzalez	Sammy Sosa
CF	Ken Griffey, Jr.	Bernie Williams
C	Ivan Rodriguez	Mike Piazza
P	Greg Maddux	Clemens, Glavine
		Smoltz, Johnson
		Rivera, Hoffman
		Cone, Pettite

Reaction to the team has been very well received. However, there is a cloud of concern hanging over New York today. No one has ever seen the Martians play. The Martians have scouted Earth for 100 years, studying our players, our managers, our fields and even our fans. We know nothing about them, except their first names. If we win, baseball is back… better than ever. If we lose, baseball, like our spirit, will be lost forever. GOOD LUCK.

Headlines of newspapers across the Earth:

BOSTON GLOBE **EARTH TO PLAY MARS** **NO RED SOX NAMED TO TEAM** Ted Williams to throw out the first ball.	*MOSCOW PRESS* **MARS FAVORED TO BEAT EARTH** **MARTIANS INVITED TO BALLET** **AS GUESTS OF KREMLIN**
LONDON NEWS EUROPEAN SOCCER LEAGUE OFFICIALS MEET IN PRIVATE SESSION TO DISCUSS EXPANSION INTO U.S.A.	*WORLD NEWS* ELVIS PLAYS FOR MARTIANS AS BACK-UP CATCHER

L. A. TIMES

O.J. SIMPS0N TRIAL CONTINUES

CHAPTER SEVEN

Tuesday, July 11, 2000

5:30 p.m.

It was just two hours before game time. The pre-game hype was the equivalent of a Super Bowl and a Presidential Election combined. Ever since the Martians had landed on Sunday, almost every national radio and television station played tribute to some aspect of this colossal event: interviews with fans, players, heads of state, biographies of the greatest players, tours of the Hall of Fame, pictures of Yankee Stadium from every conceivable angle, the history of baseball and its traditions, rules of the game and changes throughout the years, the Martians' baseball league(s), speculation as to who would score first, how to pitch to the Martians, scientific advantages/disadvantages, the banners that hang in Yankee Stadium, the impact on Americans if the All-Stars lost, how stocks may be affected, and on and on.

The most curious news segment, however, was by Pete Wisdom, the conservative political radio talk show host. He postulated that the Martians were not really Martians, but a political ploy by Democrats to improve the morale of the country and to restore peace to the World. The Democrats, the popular Wisdom cried, would not get away with this. Eight years in the White House was long enough.

By 7:30 p.m., EDT, the public address announcer at Yankee Stadium, Don Shephard, introduced the names of the players of both teams. The Martians, in their red and black team uniforms, stood on the third base line. The Earth All-Stars, in their individual team uniforms, stood on the first base line. The Martians' anthem was played first, with their red and black flag now flying alongside the flags of every nation on Earth. The American, Canadian and an international anthem followed.

Names of all the Hall of Famers were announced, with many in attendance. Stan Musial and Ted Williams' names were announced last. They were the honorary captains of the Earth team. Stan "the man" and Teddy Ballgame threw out the first balls of the game, much to the delight of the fans on Earth and Mars.

At 7:45 p.m., the Earth All-Stars took the field to the melody of "We Are The World."

The battlefield was set.

CHAPTER EIGHT

July 11, 2000

Game Time

Security at Yankee Stadium had never been so tight. Over 1,000 of NYC's finest volunteered for crowd control, both inside and outside the park. Metal detectors were installed at every entrance. Cars could not be parked within 100 yards of the Stadium. No beer was served. Tailgating was forbidden. Breathalyzers were given to all patrons. Children under five were prohibited. The first five rows of the first and third base lines were left empty to avoid any confrontation between fans and Martians over foul balls. The Pope mobile was flown in to be used for the Martians' bullpen. Plate glass was placed in front of the Martians' dugout to avoid any thrown objects. Security nets were installed in the outfield to prevent any fans from reaching over the fence to obstruct a ball in play. Radios, telephones and hand-held cameras were banned. Tickets were free, but were distributed on a who-you-know basis. No dignitaries were present in case of any disturbance – before, during or after the contest.

At 7:45 p.m., Tuesday, July 11th, 55,000 fans stood clapping, yelling, chanting and screaming for their "home" team. At homes, taverns, restaurants and open-air theaters around the globe, five billion inhabitants of Earth were affixed to their televisions and radios, hoping and praying that their lives, first and foremost, would remain basically unchanged, and secondly, that Earth would kick some Martian butt.

Back on Mars, the Martians were watching the game through the Hubble Telescope, feeling extremely confident that the Earthlings would lose the game, their composure and their spirit. Earth would then become Mars' minor-league playground.

Inside the stadium, banners spread across the facade of the Stadium: MARTIANS GO HOME; STICK IT TO THE MARTIANS; WHERE HAVE YOU GONE, JOE DIMAGGIO? – TO MARS?; EARTH – KICK MARS' BUTT (IF THEY HAVE ONE). There were over 100 banners that told the Martians where to go and how bad they were going to lose.

One banner, blowing in the right field corner, summarized the true feelings of all Americans: GOD HELP US IF WE LOSE!

CHAPTER NINE

July 11, 2000

Game Time

Instead of returning to the dugout, the Martians walked slowly from the third base line, in unison, to center field. No one knew what they were doing or exactly where they were going. Security guards all drew their firearms in anticipation of something happening. The Martians reached the center field fence, placed their arms around one another and omitted a high-pitched sound, lasting 20 seconds. The crowd was silent in wonder. The television cameras followed their every move. It became apparent that the Martians were... honoring Monument Park, the greatest Yankees of all time. They were reading the plaques and monuments honoring Ruth, Gehrig, Stengel, Mantle, DiMaggio, Huggins, Martin and Munson. Once the crowd realized what was going on, they gave the Martians a standing ovation. NYC fans are truly the most knowledgeable baseball fans.

CHAPTER TEN

Wednesday, July 12, 2000

THE NEW YORK NEWS

GAME I – YANKEE STADIUM

Babe Ruth, Ty Cobb, Lou Gehrig, Tris Speaker, Honus Wagner, Jackie Robinson, Cy Young and Walter Johnson are officially turning over in their graves. Excedrin Headache #150: Utter humiliation. The greatest of all time watched in despair as the Martians destroyed the Earth All-Stars, 15-0. The defeat was so one-sided, so unexpected, that the 55,000 fans in attendance at Yankee Stadium cheered when the game was finally over so that the bleeding could stop. The final box score was a clear indication of the magnitude of the defeat.

	HITS	RUNS	ERRORS
MARTIANS:	15	15	0
EARTH:	0	0	0

Not one Earth All-Star reached base: no walks, no hits, no errors. Sandy, the Martian pitcher, pitched a truly perfect game: 81 pitches, all strikes. No foul balls. Sandy's fast ball was clocked at 110 miles per hour. His curve broke four feet from the pitcher's mound to home plate, while traveling only 90 mph. As announced, Sandy was an ambidextrous two-armed pitcher. Pinch hitters were redundant. Every pitch was perfect. It was baseball surgery at its best.

As for the Martian hitters, it was T-Ball without the "T." The first 15 batters reached base and scored. The score was 15-0 before an out was recorded. There was not one missed pitch. There were no foul balls. There were, however, four singles, 2 doubles, 2 triples and 7 home runs, with five into "the porch" in right field. One home run was measured at 600 feet, far eclipsing the previous long of 565 feet, hit by the Mick. It all seemed like child's play for the Martians.

After the Martians scored their 15 runs, the team met with Casey, their manager, in a huddle in the dugout. After the meeting, every hit ball was grounded to either third or short, resulting in an easy out at first. The Martians seemingly allowed the Earth All-Stars to get them out to move the game along faster. At least the agony didn't last forever. The House that Ruth Built was on the verge of collapse – forever.

*****

After the game, the managers were required to attend a press conference. Casey addressed the world first:

"We have waited a very long time for the opportunity to play against the Earth's All-Stars. We have practiced many hours in preparing for this momentous occasion. I am very proud of my players and hope our beloved Mars is proud of them, too."

"I apologize for the lopsided score of the game. I told my players not to try as hard after we scored 15 runs. I hoped that your All- Stars would score some runs to make the game competitive, but unfortunately, they were unable to do so. So, I propose that the next two games be forfeited to avoid any further embarrassment."

Bobby Cox was about to jump across the table and strangle Casey. Only the reality that an inter-galactic war may result held him back. His comments were eloquent, but direct. "The Martians were a better team today. A much superior team, all around. Their pitching was supernatural; their hitting phenomenal. Their fielding is unknown because we didn't hit one ball. From all indications, however, I'm sure that their defense is also superb."

"As far as our team is concerned, we have the most talented team of players this generation of stars can offer. We have never seen fast balls and curve balls like we saw today. We did not know what we were up against. The Martians had the element of surprise – we knew nothing about them. They scouted us for over a century, even assuming our greatest players' names. They knew how to pitch to every one of our players. It was a work of art orchestrated to perfection.

I, as well as the All-Stars, have great respect for their abilities. However, we will never quit. Our baseball tradition is more important to me, to our players, and to our country than anything else. Baseball is more than our national pastime. It is a way of life – a reminder of a game that time has forgotten – of an era that equated baseball with heroes and legends. We will continue that legacy. Our goal is to win, to regain our place as the best team in the world."

"Those of you who are watching or listening to me tonight, remember this: Baseball is not measured by wins and losses. Baseball is measured by the hundreds of thousands of youngsters who play the game until dusk settles on the field, who listen to their favorite teams at 11:00 p.m. pretending to sleep, by the cheers of the fans for a great play by the opposing team. Baseball is and always will be a part of our lives."

The two managers shook hands. Years of battles were locked in that handshake. Bobby Cox made every effort to squeeze Casey's hand as tightly as possible. Casey only smiled. He knew that there was nothing the All-Stars could do that he was not prepared for already. Nothing at all!

CHAPTER ELEVEN

July 11, 2000

Game Time

The Crestview All-Star team gathered at Joni's house, eagerly anticipating the start of the new World Series. It was not unusual for the whole team to gather at Joni's house to watch a game – her dad was the team coach. The players simply told their parents that Coach was having a strategy session at his house. The parents knew exactly where to find them – 15 CRESTVIEW DRIVE – and exactly when their kids would be home. Coach was convinced that, by watching the pros play and by analyzing their every move, the players improved and the team solidified. As the Crestview All-Stars watched their idols play on television, the kids yelled out, "bunt," "steal," "pitch out," "hit and run," "pick off," etc. Since the All-Stars were undefeated, no one disagreed with Coach's approach.

Joni's living room was a miniature baseball field. The television was "home plate." The sofa (large enough for two adults and one child or four kids) was the pitcher's mound.

Two oversized chairs were first and third base. Second base was an elevated director's chair, reserved for Coach. The rest of the team piled on the floor between the "bases," getting the best view possible. The outfield was comprised of three tables: left (drinks), center (snacks) and right (sandwiches). The bathrooms were under the exit signs on both sides of the "diamond." The numerous trophies won by the All-Stars adorned the shelves, which circled the playing field like bleachers. It was a constant reminder of the team's success.

The Crestview All-Stars were 13 to 17 year old boys and girls who played in the North Central Babe Ruth League. They were league champs three years running, ever since Joni, at age 13, became the dominant pitcher in the league. The team had 12 players:

Shawn - 1st	Mike - OF	David - C
Ellis - 2nd	Stan - OF	Eric - C
Glenn - SS	Patti - OF	Joni - P
Miguel – 3rd	Pedro- OF	Carlos - P

The team had become a family over the past three years. The players respected one another. There were no "celebrities" on this team. They each knew the secret to success: play hard, know your own strengths and weaknesses, know your opposition, know the field, know the rules and play as a team. Chemistry was the key. Each player knew exactly where to play on every play. For example, when Joni is ahead of the batter 1 ball, 2 strikes with 2 outs, and no runners on base, the players on her team knew what the next pitch was going to be, its location and positioned themselves correctly on the field. Coach took great pride in transforming the All-Stars into an All-Star Team.

Game 1 ended at 9:05. It took 80 minutes, including commercials, for the Martians to destroy the beloved Earth All-Stars. No one at Joni's house had been prepared for this. A loss was possible, but how do you recover from a destruction of global proportions? The snacks, drinks and sandwiches were untouched. The bathrooms were never used. No one yelled "down in front" during the entire game. The best way to describe the mood was shock and disbelief. For the first time, every member of the Crestview All-Star Team feared that Sunday, July 16, 2000, could be the last time baseball would ever be played on Earth.

As the room cleared, Coach feverishly took notes on Game 1. That night, Joni and Coach mapped a strategy that could change the course of history – baseball history, forever.

CHAPTER TWELVE

July 12, 2000

Newspapers from around the world after game one:

BOSTON GLOBE	MOSCOW PRESS
NEW PLANS FOR FENWAY UNDERWAY **Outdoor mall suggested** **Council to take vote**	RUSSIA CHANGES FLAG IN HONOR OF MARTIANS Bat and ball replaces hammer and sickle
LONDON NEWS	WORLD NEWS
GERMANY CHALLENGES MARS TO SOCCER MATCH Martians decline: too much running around	**1ST INTER-GALACTIC CHILD BORN TO N.Y.C. WOMAN** Little "Yogi " looks just like Papa

L. A. TIMES
<u>MISSING KNIFE FOUND IN</u>

<u>ATLANTA</u>
Martians Center of Probe
Conspiracy Theory Investigated

CHAPTER THIRTEEN

July 14, 2000

Preview of Game 2

The Baseball Commissioner's Office was once again barraged with telephone calls, mail, faxes, e-mail – everyone had an opinion on how to beat the Martians and who to select for the second game. By Friday morning, the Earth All-Stars for Game 2 were selected by a combined vote of Cox, Torre, Lasorda and the Commissioner himself. The panel concluded that it didn't particularly matter who played against the Martians, but rather how in this world (galaxy) would Earth begin to discover Mars' weaknesses?! All of the Earth All-Stars were of comparable talent, but none apparently as good as the worst player on the Martians team, whoever that may be. If the Earth All-Stars could not hit Sandy or Bob, or if Earth's pitchers could not get Mars' hitters out, then Earth would always lose. Trick plays were meaningless. Cox, Torre and Lasorda, who had a combined 100 years of baseball wisdom, were without answers.

Since the Martians didn't care how many players were on Earth's roster, the team kept the original dream team (?) and added 10 additional players (1 pitcher, 9 hitters) from All-Star teams from Japan, Mexico, Puerto Rico, the Caribbean Islands and South America. At the very least, it was the right thing to do. Now, it was truly an "Earth" All-Star team.

Cox, Torre and Lasorda called every living Hall of Famer for a video conference from Los Angeles. The Earth All-Star team also was present for the brainstorming session. There were only four hours left until game time. No one wanted to play an "all or nothing" third game. If they couldn't figure out the Martians by Game 2, what would be the purpose of Game 3? Thoughts of a forfeit crossed the minds of even the best players.

The Martians were having a team meeting of their own, on board their Mother Ship. Casey, as always, was doing all the talking. "We have an opportunity that no other generation of Martians has ever had: the opportunity to dominate Earth without a single drop of blood. Once we win the next two games, baseball will be history. The word "baseball" will be an answer to a trivia question in Trivial Pursuit: What game was last played on July16, 2000? Not only are we the dominant team physically, but we have trained and prepared for these games for the last 100 years. The Earth All-Stars are weak – just like the inhabitants of Earth. We have been selected by our Supreme Commander to represent our world. We are the fruits of our parents' sacrifices and labors. We will not fail. Not only must we win, but our victories must be increasingly dramatic. We must break the spirit of the Earth All-Stars, as well as their fans. Those who hold these men as heroes and legends – the children – must learn to worship us. After the Earth loses game 2, I will call upon the children of Earth to support us – and not their pitiful All-Stars. **Our Conquest of Earth begins.**"

CHAPTER FOURTEEN

July 14, 2000

The video conference lasted two hours (noon to 2 p.m.). Unfortunately, the telecast had an uninvited guest. After observing Earth's baseball for over a century, the Martians were certainly not going to stop now.

The Pitchers

The message delivered by Tom Seaver, Whitey Ford, Bob Gibson, Sandy Koufax and Nolan Ryan was clear: "Keep the Martians off balance. Don't make every pitch perfect. Throw some at their feet, head, arms – make them uncomfortable. Walk a few... see how they run the bases – their legs appear to be "human." We have lots of pitchers – so take chances. Since we know nothing about how to pitch against them, keep one thing in mind – pitch to your strengths." Laughter broke out in the Martian clubhouse.

The Catchers

Yogi Berra, Johnny Bench and Carlton Fisk offered these words of wisdom to the catchers: "Break the concentration of the hitters. Constantly talk to them. Tell them what pitch to expect. Keep moving the target – remember they have eyes in back of their heads. Keep kicking up dirt – they have no facial hair – maybe the dust will bother their vision." Yogi had one final comment – "ask them if they drink Yoo Hoo up on Mars."

The Hitters

Rod Carew, Willy Mays, Lou Brock, Hank Aaron, Tony Oliva, Carl Yastrzemski, Ted Williams, Stan Musial, Ernie Banks and Phil Rizzuto gave their advice on how to hit Sandy (or Bob):

- "Shorten your swing and just make contact. Let's see how they field."
- "Go for the homers – one good old-fashioned long ball may break their confidence."
- "Holy Cow, bunt, bunt and bunt some more. Let's see how fast those legs can move and how accurate those long arms can throw."
- "If we get on base, take big leads – attempt to steal as often as possible. If Sandy pitches, get him to throw to first as much as possible. He's pitching on two days' rest. Even though he's pitching with both arms, he must be a little tired."
- "Crowd the plate – get hit by the pitch – just get on base – break their concentration."

- "Go for hits up the middle – see how well their pitchers field. Maybe a line drive will hit their leg or some other part of their body."
- "Keep a good distance from the plate – get full extension."
- "Crouch – cut the strike zone in half."
- "Stand back in the box on fast balls – stand ahead of the plate on curve balls..."

The video conference ended with Casey taking more notes than the Earth All-Stars and their coaches.

*****

Coach, Joni and the Crestview All-Stars watched replays of Game 1 a dozen times between Tuesday night and Friday afternoon. If there were any weaknesses, Coach was convinced his team could find it. The first thing that became clear to all the players was that the Martians were almost all identical: same height, same long arms, same size legs, same wide feet and no hair on their heads. If they were able to develop a strategy to stop one of them, then it could conceivably stop all of them. Secondly, no one knew if the Martians could run, play defense or if they were baseball smart. Instead of assuming a "yes" answer to all of these questions, the team concluded "maybe not." Why? If the Martians had observed Earth for 100 years, they knew exactly how each pitcher throws, how each batter hits and how each manager manages. They know what to expect at every moment. They won't know what to expect if we do the opposite.

The team was convinced that they were on the right track. But there was so little time remaining before Game 2. How could they figure it out if the best minds in baseball had been over-matched?

David, the team's catcher, shouted, "Coach, even if we are able to slow down their offense, how are we going to hit their pitching? Sandy's fastball is 110 mph and his curve is wicked. Who knows how fast Bob or Goose are?" Coach had given this a lot of thought. Sandy, the two-armed wonder, was the key to the Martians' success. None of the team's ideas so far impacted on his speed or accuracy. On replay, Sandy was a combination of Walter Johnson and Luis Tiant. His dual windmill arm swings were extremely effective and distracting. His hesitation delivery lulled batters into waiting too long to begin their swing. Then – in a flash – the arm "whipped" the ball at 110 mph into the catcher's glove. Sandy was truly a pitching machine. Making the bats lighter or the balls heavier crossed Coach's mind, but that would change the game. The integrity of baseball had to be maintained.

As the team continued its meeting, ABC flashed a picture of Dodgers' Stadium. It was a picture-perfect day in Los Angeles, temperature in the mid-80s, with a light breeze. The field itself was flawless: the infield diamond was manicured to perfection, the outfield grass trimmed in a crisscrossed fashion, with hardly a pebble in sight. Except for artificial turf, the stadium had remained unchanged for the past 38 years. Suddenly, Coach knew how to beat the Martians. He gathered his team closer. For the first time in three days, hope reappeared on the faces of the Crestview All-Star team. But, how were they going to get this information to the

Commissioner of Baseball? The game was set to begin in a half hour.

*****

At 4:35 p.m., Pacific Daylight Time, the Earth All-Stars and the Martians took the field for the playing of the anthems. The Martians were the home team for Game 2 and took the playing field first. The Martian dugout was empty except for Casey, Bob and Goose. Casey was going to give Goose some "mop up" work in the eighth and ninth to prove that the Martians were more than a "one-pitcher team." Meanwhile, Bob was being saved for the third game, if necessary. In the Earth All-Stars' dugout, 25 players filled the dugout to capacity. Cox had an additional 10 players in the bullpen. The baseball gurus decided to have each pitcher pitch one inning to see who had the best stuff against the Martians. As for trying to hit Sandy, it was clear from Game 1 that he always threw strikes – so the players were going to get their cuts early and often. They agreed to stand deep in the batter's box if they expected a fastball and ahead of the plate if they expected a curve. Each and every player believed that making contact was a victory. However, no one expected a win – not after the nightmare of Game 1.

*****

The Coach's e-mail, faxes and telephone messages lay unread among the thousands that were stacked on the Commissioner's desk.

CHAPTER FIFTEEN

July 14, 2000

8:00 p.m.

"Good evening. This is Bob Costas. I'm standing in front of the Earth All-Star dugout. As the lightning and thunder lit up the evening sky outside Los Angeles, the hope of playing baseball for millions of kids faded today as the Martians proved again to be the dominant team, destroying the Earth All-Stars 18-2. The game began and ended on encouraging notes for the Earth All-Stars. Earth, batting first, scored off the Martians' ace pitcher, Sandy, in the very first inning. Carlos Baerga led off with a bunt down the third base line. It was the first time anyone on the Earth All-Stars had hit a pitch by Sandy, let alone for a base hit. The Martian's third baseman, Mike, fielded the ball cleanly and threw a strike to first, but Baerga beat the throw. The crowd cheered wildly as Baerga took a dramatic lead off first, challenging Sandy and the Martian's catcher, Yogi. On a 0-1 count to Gwynn, Baerga broke for second base. Yogi whipped the ball to Ozzie, the shortstop covering the bag, but once again Baerga beat the throw. Speed was clearly a weapon the Earth All-Stars could use against the almighty Martians. With no outs and an 0-2 count on Gwynn, Baerga broke for third base. Gwynn laid down a perfect bunt, protecting the runner while moving him to third with one out. Ken Griffey, Jr. stepped to the plate. On the first pitch from Sandy, a 105 mph fastball, Junior ripped a long line drive into right field. The ball was destined for the bullpen when Babe, using his right arm as leverage, jumped and stretched his oversized limbs over the wall for the greatest catch this baseball fan ever saw. The score was 1-0, but Babe saved what could have been a big inning. After the first inning, it was clear that Sandy was hittable, speed important, and the Martians could play defense."

"The rest of the game was a near repeat of Game 1, especially the final score. The Martians were a hitting machine, stroking 25 hits over 8 innings. They also received 10 walks, with most of them occurring in the first three innings. Normally flawless in his accuracy, Maddox walked four of the first five batters he faced. The Martians took the lead 5-1 after the first inning. The game was marred by verbal altercations between Rodriguez, the Earth All-Stars' catcher, and several of the Martian hitters. No one was ejected, but the frustration of the All-Stars was evident."

"Despite the second lopsided score in three days, Game 2 did show marked improvement over Game 1. The All-Stars had 7 hits, 5 of which were bunts, and 1 home run. The home run was a mammoth home run by Mark McGwire. It was hit as hard and as far as any ball hit by the Martians. The blast came off Goose, who worked the ninth inning, giving Sandy some much-needed rest."

Gary H. Goldberg

"The Martians' overall defense had an opportunity to show its worth. Sandy struck out seven, and while not as overpowering as in Game 1, proved more than effective. Mike, the third baseman, was excellent at the hot corner, fielding ten bunts – all flawlessly. The Martians showed agility and speed in the field. Yogi threw out four would-be base stealers."

"Earth's pitchers had better success against the Martians than in Game 1, if you call giving up 18 runs a success. Three times the Martians went down in order. Four times the Martians failed to score in an inning. Only two home runs were hit off Earth's pitching. If the pitchers were attempting to keep the Martians off-balance, they were partially successful. Earth's pitchers threw 200 pitches over eight innings, with no less than fifteen pitches per inning. The first pitch to each hitter was never a strike. The pitches were mostly inside, from the shoes to the shoulders. Don Drysdale and Bob Gibson would have been proud. In fact, three Martians were hit by pitches. They showed no emotions when plunked, simply spitting tobacco at the catcher's feet. One final note for the game: the Martians wore protective eye gear while batting. Several times the home plate umpire called time to allow the dust around home plate to settle. Although visibility was poor, the Martians never asked for time-out."

"The Earth All-Stars have one more game remaining – this Sunday – at a time and location still yet to be announced. They must find a way to overcome the Martians' superiority in pitching and hitting. If they fail, Sunday may very well be baseball's finale. This is Bob Costas from Dodgers Stadium. See you Sunday."

CHAPTER SIXTEEN

July 14, 2000

Earth All-Stars Locker Room

Losing by 16 runs never makes for a joyous locker room. But, with one game remaining on the "schedule," fingers were not pointed to any player or coach. Instead, a numbness had started to settle in.

The players sat in front of their lockers, dressed in their battle gear, showing signs of exhaustion and fatigue. Cox addressed his players: "We have lost two straight games by a total score of 33-2. I've got to attend this press conference in five minutes and tell the world that I am confident that Sunday – 36 hours from now – the outcome will be different, that Sunday we will not lose. That Sunday will not be the last day of baseball for our planet. I've got to convince the millions of kids who look up to us that we will not let them down, again. How the hell am I supposed to do that?"

The locker room went silent. All eyes were facing downward. The players didn't even notice the Commissioner of Baseball enter the room.

CHAPTER SEVENTEEN

July 14, 2000

Martians' Locker Room

The Martians' locker room was filled with high-5s, low-5s, chest-thumping and the more traditional thumbshakes. Casey's entrance put a quick end to the celebration.

"Our mission is not complete. We must remain focused on our goal. There is one more game to play. I have no doubt that we will be victorious, but the Earth All-Stars were successful today in scoring runs and occasionally getting us out. We must not let them gain confidence. I will once again call upon Earth to forfeit the last game. If they choose to play, we must crush them. Let them forever know that we are their superiors."

Casey left for the press conference carrying a small attaché. Inside was the **Downfall of Earth**.

CHAPTER EIGHTEEN

Press Conference – Game 2

July 14, 2000

At 8:30 PST (11:30 p.m. EDT), the post-game press conference began. As before, Casey addressed the media and the world first.

"People of Earth. Martians are simple beings. We have the same hopes and dreams as the inhabitants of Earth. Although we may look different, do not judge us on the color of our skin or on our outward appearance. Rather, judge us on our abilities and our accomplishments. Do not fear us, but welcome us to your world."

"Over the past several days, our best athletes have shared the baseball field with your world's best players. Although it was your world that invented the game, the student has become the master. Your best players would not even be selected to play in our minor leagues."

"After the first game, I called upon you to forfeit Games 2 and 3 to avoid any further embarrassment. You gallantly chose to play Game 2, with hopes of redemption. We respected your desire, but believed your efforts to be futile. We were correct. We call upon you once again to forfeit your final game and concede victory to us. If this were war, you surely would not risk losing more lives if the outcome was certain defeat. Please consider our offer seriously."

One of the rookie reporters jumped to his feet. "Casey, to what advantage would it be for Earth to forfeit Game 3? Whether we lose or forfeit, baseball will no longer be played here on Earth. At least if we play, we still have a chance of winning."

The other reporters echoed the rookie's sentiments. Casey reached for his attaché and placed it on the tabletop. The reporters were unsure whether to be scared or simply inquisitive. Either way, Casey was once again prepared.

"I have a proposition for your world to consider. If you play Game 3 and win, we shall leave your world immediately. If you lose Game 3, baseball will be eliminated from your way of life. If you forfeit, however, we will allow you to continue to play baseball under the following conditions:

    a) The Baseball Hall of Fame will be replaced with the Martian Hall of Fame. Since none of your best players can compete with our best, all current members of the Hall of Fame will be replaced by Martian players.

    b) All baseball articles and memorabilia – cards, bats, balls, autographs, pictures, videos, radio broadcasts, t-shirts, pants, spikes – must be destroyed or exchanged before game time, Sunday.

c) I will authorize distribution of Martian baseball articles and memorabilia. I have brought samples of playing cards, t-shirts, caps, bats and pictures. Distribution centers will be set up around the world, displaying the Martian colors, red and black, and our logo, a black bat with a red sphere. Destruction centers will also be established, with receipts given to those willingly participating."

"And, if we don't willingly participate?" Casey's comments were interrupted by the rookie reporter.

Casey responded, this time with anger in his voice. "We will work closely with your governments to make sure every person has the opportunity to exchange their baseball articles for Martian artifacts. Anyone caught using or wearing Earth-related baseball articles will be in violation of the agreement and subject to penalties."

The Baseball Commissioner quickly stepped in. "Casey, let me make our position absolutely clear to you, to the citizens of Earth watching this broadcast, and to the inhabitants of Mars. I will not allow you or anyone else to threaten our way of life. We have faced tyranny and oppression before, and each time our democratic way of life prevailed. Second, we are not quitters. Until the final out of the last inning is recorded, victory remains possible. The inhabitants of Earth have a resilient quality that never dies. We will not forfeit Game 3."

A loud, boisterous cheer arose from the media present at the conference.

"As to the logistics of Game 3, we will play Game 3 at 1:00 on Sunday afternoon, July 16. The identities of our players will remain secret until game time. The game will be played in Massachusetts at a field to be determined. There will be no fans allowed at the contest. There will be no television broadcast, only radio. No other press will be invited. The only people allowed at the game will be the umpires, players, trainers, paramedics, managers and radio personnel. We will inform you one hour before game time of the specific location of Game 3. Do you have any questions?"

Casey responded, "I have no questions. I truly feel sorry for all the children of Earth who love baseball. In less than 40 hours, baseball will be banned, and they will have only you to blame."

CHAPTER NINETEEN

Earth Locker Room

15 minutes earlier

The Commissioner stood tall among the disheartened All-Stars. He looked around the room, carefully analyzing the faces of the "best" players on Earth.

"On Sunday, Earth may very well play its last game of baseball. We hoped it would not come down to one final game, but the Martians have proven to be a truly formidable opponent. In case we lose on Sunday, I am asking each Major League player to return to their home-town, to their roots. At high noon, one hour before game time, go to your favorite field from your childhood and bring all the youngsters from the neighborhood with you. Spend time with them... they are the future of baseball, the future of our world. Baseball is a game for the ages. Let all the kids, from ages 3 to 93, play together on the same field. Bring your wives, girlfriends, children and parents. Let them play and enjoy the game, maybe for their first time or for the thousandth. Teach them.

Play with them. Have fun again. No matter what happens Sunday, I'm proud of each and every one of you."

As the Commissioner left the locker room, he passed out a typed 3x5 index card. On it was the recipe for Mars' defeat.

CHAPTER TWENTY

Friday Night – July 14, 2000

Midnight

By Midnight (EDT), every Major League baseball team had been informed of the Commissioner's request. Thousands of Major and Minor League players representing all 50 states and Mexico, Japan, Korea, the Caribbean Islands, Cuba, Venezuela, and Puerto Rico, made arrangements to fly home on Saturday and play baseball with their community on Sunday morning. The third Sunday in July would forever be known as "Community Baseball Day." Even if baseball was never played again, the memory of baseball and its meaning to family and community would never be forgotten.

CHAPTER TWENTY-ONE

<u>Friday Night – July 14, 2000</u>
<u>7:30 EDT</u>

The Crestview All-Star Team gathered at Coach's house for the second game of the World Series between Earth and Mars. The room was filled with excitement and anticipation. The players knew that their heroes were going to lose. It didn't matter. The game was on television, but the audio was turned off. Although the All-Stars' eyes were on the game, their ears – and their hearts – were on Coach. He was not in his director's chair. He was on the phone with the Commissioner of Baseball. Coach was on a mission.

CHAPTER TWENTY-TWO

Friday Night at 11:15 p.m. EDT

Mother Ship

"They are fools. Every one of them, especially that Commissioner," yelled Casey as he conducted his post-game team meeting. Casey walked towards the monitor and turned on the surveillance camera. On the screen was the Earth's locker room after the game. He turned on the audio as the Martians watched the Commissioner enter the locker room. As the Commissioner concluded his speech, Casey and his teammates looked on in suspense as the Commissioner passed out index cards to each of the players and coaches. Casey re-focused the monitor to allow for a close-up look.

Dear Casey,

Your team looked good in goggles. See you Sunday.

Casey was speechless.

CHAPTER TWENTY-THREE

Saturday, July 15, 2000

8:00 a.m.

Coach had one day to prepare his team for tomorrow's game. As they did before all big games, Coach and Joni walked Crestview Park early that morning to discuss strategy. Although they had barely slept for days, both remained sharp and alert. As Joni smoothed out the dirt on the pitcher's mound, Coach laid out the time schedule for the next 24 hours.

"At 10:00 a.m., we'll meet at the school gym for an indoor practice. We'll borrow the pitching machine to get used to the speed of Mars' pitchers. We'll practice our bunting, stealing and fielding indoors, as well. We know the Martians will be scanning every field in Massachusetts to figure out where the game will be played and who will be their competition. We must keep our identities a secret until noon tomorrow. By then it will be too late for them to plan any strategy against us."

"At 1:00 p.m., we'll again review tapes of Games 1 and 2. At 5:00 p.m., we'll meet at the Town Hall for a community supper in anticipation of Community Baseball Day tomorrow. By 9:00 p.m., we'll be asleep and the Martians will be driving themselves crazy."

"Dad," Joni whispered, "what if we don't win? What if our plan backfires?"

"Joni, whether we win or lose tomorrow, Sunday will be the most memorable day ever for baseball. Millions of kids will be playing ball alongside the greatest players of our day. The adults will be in the stands, rooting for their children and grandchildren. At 1:00 p.m., the games will stop. All ears will be focused on Phil Rizzuto calling the game. Through his voice, the world will watch baseball the way it was meant to be watched: in our mind's eye. And when we win, baseball will be back, stronger than ever."

Joni gave her dad a big hug. Father and daughter walked home, smiling, arm-in-arm.

As they slowly strolled home, Crestview Park lay waiting in the darkness. Home field never smelled so sweet.

CHAPTER TWENTY-FOUR

Saturday, July 15, 2000

Mother Ship

Casey paced the traveling locker room like an expectant father of triplets. His strategy was not exactly working as planned. Sure, his team had easily defeated the mighty Earth All-Stars in the first two games. But he expected more fan support. There were only a handful of demonstrations around the globe protesting the decision to play Game 3. The Distribution and Destruction Centers had been set up, but since Game 3 was going to be played, use of the facilities was minimal. It appeared that Earth would rather stop playing baseball altogether than play it on Mars' terms.

"So be it. Let Earth pay the ultimate price for their stubbornness."

The monitors in the control room were scanning Massachusetts for baseball activity. Hundreds of Little League games dotted the landscape. Since the Commissioner had announced

Community Baseball Day for Sunday, the large number of games played was not unexpected.

Casey was unable to determine the identity of their Game 3 opponents. All efforts to gather information by monitoring Earth's communication systems were unsuccessful. The Office of the Commissioner of Baseball was in communication with the President of the United States, team owners and the media. All the transmissions, however, were about Community Baseball Day and the importance of family. No one was talking about Game 3.

Casey and his teammates had come a long way to prove their dominance over Earth. His mission was to get Earth to succumb to Mars through its sheer athletic dominance. Once defeated, Earth's spirit would crumble. But even after losing the first two games, Earth's spirit appeared stronger than ever. Casey was prepared for every possible diversion. Was he prepared, however, to play a third and decisive game against an unknown opponent on an unknown field, led by an unknown manager?

Casey decided that the key to his search was discovering the identity of the team's manager. He programmed their computer to locate every former major/minor league player/manager/coach who lived in Massachusetts. Casey believed that the coach probably had his own baseball team. After the Commissioner's announcement on Friday night, no major leaguer was going to be available to play on Sunday. The manager had to live in Massachusetts since the decision had only been made within the past 24 hours.

Casey soon realized that he was looking in the wrong direction. Casey re-programmed the surveillance system for any transmissions to the Baseball Commissioner on Friday, July 14th from Massachusetts. Casey was on an intergalactic roll.

CHAPTER TWENTY-FIVE

Commissioner of Baseball's Office

Saturday, July 15, 2000

The Commissioner had been a baseball man for over 30 years. His love of the game dated back to the 1940s, when he had watched the Giants at the Polo Grounds. Although he had previously owned a major league team, he never got involved in player negotiations or day-to-day managerial decisions. He always left that to the "field generals."

As he sat in his office, the Baseball Commissioner scanned over 100 pictures, articles and memorabilia that lined his mini Wall of Fame. The Wall included some of the game's greatest moments: Babe Ruth's 60th home run, Lou Gehrig's farewell, Jackie Robinson's first major league game, Don Larson's perfect game in the 1956 World Series, Bobby Thompson's shot heard around the world, Carlton Fisk waving to the ball to stay fair in Game 6 of 1975 World Series, Willie Mays' over-the-shoulder catch in the '54 World Series, Bucky Dent's home run against the Red Sox in the 1978 playoff game, and Mark McGwire's 62nd home run.

The headlines of every major newspaper across the United States and possibly the world had baseball as its front-page lead story. Its only story. The Commissioner had the Martians to thank for the sudden overnight worldwide popularity of the game.

If baseball could survive Sunday's game, if somehow Earth could win, the Commissioner would be viewed as the Savior of the Game. If Earth lost, however, he would be remembered as the all-time GOAT. His future and the future of the game itself lay in the hands of Coach Levy and his team of miniature All-Stars. The Commissioner took his heart medicine and closed his eyes. He kept his promise to himself – let the field generals handle the game.

CHAPTER TWENTY-SIX

Saturday, July 15, 2000

Crestview Town Hall

Crestview was a small Massachusetts town of approximately 10,000. At 5:00 p.m., Saturday, July 15th, over 1,000 members of the Crestview community joined together to celebrate Community Baseball Day on the Town Common. Most families brought enough food and beverages for themselves and for those less fortunate. Vendors roamed the grounds selling peanuts, popcorn and Cracker Jacks. Anyone who owned a baseball uniform was encouraged to wear it. A baseball poetry contest was held at 6:00 p.m. Reprints of "Casey at the Bat" were handed out to those in attendance. Baseball songs were sung spontaneously throughout the evening. At 7:30 p.m., three giant screens showed *The Natural, Field of Dreams* and *The Pride of the Yankees.*

The Crestview All-Star team dressed in their "working clothes." Coach proudly sat at the head of their table. Besides the players themselves and the Commissioner, no one, not even their parents, knew that the Crestview All-Stars were the "chosen ones" to defend Earth against the Martians.

No one noticed the All-Stars leaving the festivities at 9:00 p.m. All eyes were on James Earl Jones walking into the corn field, on Robert Redford rounding the bases with the light tower exploding all around him and Gary Cooper telling the world that he was the "luckiest man alive on the face of this Earth."

CHAPTER TWENTY-SEVEN

July 15, 2000

10:00 p.m.

Joni was not particularly religious. But like so many before her, in overwhelming times, Joni reached out for a helping Hand for guidance. "Dear God, my name is Joni Levy. We haven't talked for quite some time. The last time we spoke was 10 years ago when you invited my mommy to stay with you. Tell her I love her and miss her."

"I'm really scared about tomorrow. I know Dad says to just do my best and things will be fine, but what if we lose? I'll be letting down all the kids in the whole world. I'm only 15 years old. How can I pitch better than Maddox or Johnson? I'm not as fast or as strong as they are. Dad says you're a good listener. He says that you gave us the tools to be whoever we want to be. After Sunday, I want to be able to play baseball again. God, can you give me the tools to make that happen?" Joni started to jump back into bed, but remembered one last thought.

"P.S.: If Sparky is up there, too, rub his belly for me. He really liked that."

Coach slowly closed the door to Joni's room. He knew his daughter was a winner, even if she had doubts herself.

CHAPTER TWENTY-EIGHT

Saturday at 11:00 p.m.

Mother Ship

Casey's espionage uncovered a fax sent to the Commissioner of Baseball's office from Crestview, Massachusetts, at 4:30 (PDT) on Friday, July 14th. The fax read:

Dear Commissioner Johnson:

I have discovered the secret to beating the Martians. Please contact me as soon as possible. Use caution. They may be monitoring all calls.

> Coach George Levy
> 15 Crestview Drive
> Crestview, Massachusetts
> 508-555-2255

At 5:30 (PDT), while Game 2 was in the fourth inning, a telephone call was placed from the same address to the Commissioner of Baseball's private, unlisted cellular phone. The following conversation took place:

Baseball Commissioner: "Hello."

Coach Levy: "Commissioner, my name is George Levy. I sent you a fax an hour ago on the secret to beating the Martians. Did you get it?"

Baseball Commissioner: "I don't know. I've received thousands of faxes over the past few days. Who are you and how did you get my private number?"

Coach Levy: "Never mind that. I know how we can win. But our telephone call may be monitored."

Baseball Commissioner: "How do you know that?"

Coach Levy: "I don't know for sure, but if the Martians know all about us, then there is a good chance they've been listening and watching, very closely, for a very long time."

Baseball Commissioner: "Well, you may have a point."

Coach Levy: "Do you notice anything different about the Martians today?"

Baseball Commissioner: The Commissioner placed the telephone down and picked up his binoculars, scanning the

Martian players. "Why yes, I do. They are all wearing some kind of protective eye gear."

Coach Levy: "Rodriguez is kicking up dirt around home plate. Was he told to do that?"

Baseball Commissioner: "Yeah. It was discussed at our video conference this afternoon."

Coach Levy: "But, the Martians wore the goggles before Rodriguez started kicking up dirt."

Baseball Commissioner: "They must have heard our conference. You're right. Okay, Mr. Levy, we need to talk. But how?"

Coach Levy: "Go down to the press room and look for Samuel Adams. He has a detailed message for you. After you read it, give me a clue at the press conference if you accept my offer. I'll take it from there."

Casey was unable to locate the message from Samuel Adams. There was no one by that name in the press room. But he now knew the identity of the manager. Coach George Levy. Who is Coach Levy? The data bank was filled with information on every single minor/major league player since 1900. There was no mention of a ballplayer by the name of George Levy.

Undaunted, Casey tapped into the records of Crestview Town Hall. The census revealed that George Levy had lived at 15 Crestview Drive for 20 years, having moved there in 1980 with his wife and dog. His wife died in 1990. He has one daughter, Joni, age 15. He works as a sports psychologist. His household income is between $50,000 and $100,000. He is on the town's recreational committee and coaches a group of pint-size teenage All-Stars.

Casey knew there wasn't much time. He had discovered the identity of the manager and his opponents. He called for a meeting of his players, especially the pitching staff. Unfortunately, he did not continue his search to discover the identity of the field. The deed would have revealed that 15 Crestview Drive was adjacent to Crestview Park. Earth still maintained its home field advantage.

CHAPTER TWENTY-NINE

Sunday Morning, July 16th

Crestview Park

The Crestview All-Stars held a pre-game team practice early Sunday morning on Jackson Field. The players' parents were told that Coach wanted Crestview to be a model town for Community Baseball Day. He wanted them to practice early prior to the festivities at "high noon."

The players were dressed in their practice uniforms, light blue with orange lettering and trim. On the front of the jersey was written "Crestview" in script. Only the players' numbers appeared on the backs of the jerseys. No players' names appeared on the uniform. The Coach believed in "team victories and team defeats." Individual accomplishments were left to the statisticians.

After going through 45 minutes of fielding practice with the infielders and outfielders, Coach let each player take 10 cuts at Sandy, the nickname given to the "pitching machine." Emphasis was placed on contact and placement. Coach knew his players were not strong enough to hit homers over the Martian outfield. This game would be won one base at a time.

While the position players were taking batting practice, Coach pulled Joni and Carlos aside. "I know both of you are extremely nervous. Believe in yourself and believe in your team. I have the utmost confidence in both of you. Now, just remember..." Coach repeated the game plan that the three of them had discussed dozens of times over the past two days.

The practice session ended at around 10:00 a.m., with the team headed towards Coach's house for the traditional pre-game pancake breakfast. As they shuffled into Coach's back yard, every member of the team noticed the Mother Ship hovering overhead. It was still two hours before the Commissioner was to announce the location of the game!

CHAPTER THIRTY

Sunday, July 16<u>th</u>

Mars Mother Ship

Sandy, Bob and Goose met with Casey in the pitchers' practice room high above ground level. There were no accessible records identifying the players on Coach Levy's team. Casey knew that the players were teenagers, since the ages of the Babe Ruth League range from 13 to 17. Knowing the ages of their opponents provided Casey with enough advance information to properly prepare his pitchers.

"Bob, you're going to start today. Sandy's arms need a rest. We need to readjust your delivery for the lower and shortened strike zones. You may lose a few miles on your fastball, but we need to throw strikes." Casey instructed his pitchers to go to the practice mound in the simulation room. The simulation room was designed to duplicate the exact playing conditions of their next game. By voice command, the height of the pitcher's mound, the texture of the dirt and the hole adjacent to the pitching rubber changed. Next, the simulator projected a 3D batter in the batter's box with the catcher and umpire in their respective positions. The simulator, after projecting the batter's height, weight, arm length, stance, bat weight and length and career statistics, would then reconfigure the 3D batter. A blue zone over the plate indicated where not to pitch the hitter. A red zone indicated the ideal pitching location to get the batter out. The simulator then projected the arc best suited to get the batter out, whether by ground out, pop up or strike out. All of the information for the simulator was then downloaded into computer chips and placed into the brain stem of the pitcher. After placement, the pitcher recreated the simulator's movements to make sure that there were no problems with the program or the chips.

Casey didn't have the luxury of fully programming the simulator, since the specific scouting information on their opponents was unknown. But by readjusting the strike zone and the pitching arc, Casey was confident that no teenager could hit 100-mph fastballs.

CHAPTER THIRTY-ONE

<u>Sunday Morning, July 16th</u>

<u>Pancake Breakfast</u>

Despite the importance of the game, which was now less than three hours away, the All-Stars ate like a bunch of vultures. Forty pancakes, five pounds of fruit, two dozen eggs and three pounds of bacon were gone within 15 minutes. Coach did not want them eating too close to game time, but conditioning and nutrition were always important for a solid performance on the field. Water and protein snacks were always available during the game. The sunlight filtering into the dining room was "overshadowed" by the Mother Ship.

Knowing the location of the Mother Ship, Coach was extremely careful not to discuss game strategy. It was obvious that the Martians knew he was involved in today's final game. He surmised that they had tracked his telephone calls and faxes to the Baseball Commissioner. How much more they knew was uncertain. Coach, however, was prepared to use this opportunity to give the Martians more to think about.

"Team, listen up, I want to go over with you our game plan for this afternoon." As the Coach began his speech, the shadow of the Mother Ship which had appeared in the back yard, appeared to get bigger. "Since the Martians are clearly superior to us physically, we have to outsmart them in order for us to win. This includes wearing the appropriate protective equipment. It is going to be very hot outside, so use a lot of sunscreen, especially the outfielders. Use the honey-based sunscreen that we bought especially for today's game. Second, since the ground is hard from the lack of rainfall this summer, wear your sneakers, no spikes. Wear your extra-dark sunglasses to cut down on the glare at bat and in the field. And, most importantly, wear earmuffs to keep the mosquitoes from buzzing in your ears."

"Let's go over our signals one more time. When I rub my forehead, it means that the pitcher should throw at their heads. When I scratch my nose, it means bunt. When I adjust my pants, it means hit-and-run. When I rub the back of my neck, it means the batter has the green light, and when I rub the front of my neck, it means take the pitch. Pitchers and catchers, use the same signals that we have been using all season long. When a runner is on second base, use reverse signals."

"Above all, let's show them good sportsmanship. At the beginning of the game, before the teams are announced, go over to their players and shake their hands. Let's go out and have some fun. Let's make this game one that they will not soon forget."

CHAPTER THIRTY-TWO

Sunday, July 16th

11:00 a.m.

Community Baseball Day was baseball's finest hour. Thousands of professional athletes, active and retired, returned to their home-towns, and like the Pied Piper of Hamelin, attracted hundreds of followers to their Fields of Dreams. Sunday morning newspapers announced the details of the return of their "prodigal sons," including the location and timing of the games and clinics. Extra seating was made available for fans. Whoever wanted to play, played. Whoever wanted a handshake or autograph, got it... at no charge. Loudspeakers were set up at every field across the country to listen to "The Game."

In one hour, the Commissioner was to announce the game's location.

CHAPTER THIRTY-THREE

Sunday, July 16<u>th</u>

Noon

The Commissioner arrived in Massachusetts early Sunday morning. He had to witness, for himself, the final showdown between Earth and Mars. Arrangements were made with WFAN in New York to broadcast the game worldwide through an intricate series of hook-ups of satellites across the world. WFAN set up remotes at the direction of the Baseball Commissioner in the major cities in and surrounding Massachusetts: Boston, Worcester, Springfield, Providence, Hartford and Hyannis. The stations were all within one hour of most locations in Massachusetts.

The Commissioner arrived by helicopter in Worcester at 11:45 a.m. He made his way to the remote located at the Worcester Airport at exactly 12:00 noon. "Casey, this is Commissioner Johnson. The game will be played at Crestview Park in Crestview, Massachusetts. Look for a flashing red beacon five miles northwest from Worcester Airport." The Commissioner had not even finished his announcement, when the Martians, led by Casey, disembarked from their Mother Ship.

CHAPTER THIRTY-FOUR

Sunday, July 16th at 12:15 p.m.

Crestview Park

"Hello everybody. This is Phil Rizzuto. I will be calling the play-by-play for the game between the Martian All-Stars and the Earth All-Stars, represented by the Crestview All-Star team. It is a pleasure and an honor to be selected as the announcer for today's historic event. Let me begin by paying tribute to the memories of the late ballplayers, managers, owners, umpires and announcers who have helped create the game of baseball. A moment of silence will be taken in their honor."

"I welcome all the listeners out there taking part in Community Baseball Day today from around the nation and the world. May this be the first of many Community Baseball Days to be celebrated. The game today is being played in Crestview Park, Crestview, Massachusetts, a small town in north-central Worcester County, situated in the heart of Massachusetts, 50 miles west of Boston and 50 miles east of Springfield. It is a bright, sunny day, about 85 degrees with a slight 5- to 10-

mph breeze, blowing from left to right. It is truly a picture-perfect day for baseball."

"It is difficult to describe the dimensions of this field because there are no defining boundaries or fences. The park itself is comprised of two baseball fields, a soccer field, basketball and tennis courts, and a playground. The area residents refer to this larger field as Jackson Field and the smaller one as Yaz Field. As is typical of these types of parks, the left field in Jackson runs into right field in Yaz. The two center fields merge into one and right field in Jackson extends into a soccer/football field. In the distance are basketball and tennis courts and a playground. Due to the size of the fields and the lack of fences, there is a very good potential for inside-the-park home runs. Speed in the outfield and on the base paths will be critical."

"As I walk the field, the field itself appears to be in generally good condition. The infield is hard, with the grass about three to four inches high. Although the grass will probably slow down some hard hit balls, others may hop over the infielders' heads. The Baltimore chop is alive and well in Crestview, Massachusetts."

"The first and third base lines are well marked up to the base itself. The foul lines beyond the bags are sketchy. The foul territory extends to a line of trees on the left and to a walkway on the right. The umpires will have their work cut out for them today."

"The outfield grass appears to be similar in height and texture to the infield, but left field is barren as compared to right or center. Look for the ball to skip or to take very high bounces in left field."

"The infield dirt between the bases is rocky and uneven. Crazy bounces and bad hops will also likely occur in the infield. Holy cow, I hope the players are wearing their protective gear."

"The pitcher's mound is a little low as compared to the majors, making it more difficult for the pitchers to reach really high speeds."

"Behind home plate is a 20-foot-high cage that acts as a backstop on passed balls or wild pitches. Balls hit between home plate and the cage are in play, but foul. Balls hitting the cage or behind the cage are out of bounds. Foul territory extends from the corners of the cage to the dugouts on the first and third base lines. The dugouts are made up of two wooden benches placed together. The first and third base coaching boxes are small islands of dirt cut out of the grass in foul territory. Similarly, the on-deck circles, which are adjacent to the dugouts, are patches of dirt amidst the green grass. Behind the dugouts are aluminum stands five rows high with a maximum holding capacity of 100 to 150 fans each. Today, the stands are empty except for a handful of medical and radio personnel. On the perimeter of the park, security lines the streets, making certain no one except authorized personnel enter the park. It seems eerie that the most important game ever played, which may also be the last game ever played, has no fans in attendance."

CHAPTER THIRTY-FIVE

<u>Sunday, July 16th</u>

<u>Crestview Park</u>

"I am sitting on a raised platform, approximately 20 feet high and immediately next to the metal backstop. Both teams are now entering the playing field. HOLY COW, I have never seen anything like this before in my entire life. The Martians are wearing their now familiar red and black uniforms, but are also sporting dark sunglasses and Converse All-World sneakers. If that isn't enough, the Crestview All Star team, in their orange and blue uniforms, are also wearing dark sunglasses, Nike sneakers and, get this, ear muffs. This is unbelievable."

"The two teams are now walking across the diamond towards one another. This is truly an amazing sight: the Martians, six to seven feet tall with purple heads and long snake-like arms, are about to shake hands with the Crestview All-Stars, a bunch of teenagers, several of whom are under five feet tall. It looks like something out of one of those video games my grandchildren play. Both teams have come to a complete stop between the pitcher's mound and first base. The Crestview All-Stars, one-by-one, extend their hands to the Martians. The Martians, almost as if this was rehearsed, extend their hands in unison to their youthful opponents. The players shake hands and return to their respective benches. Maybe all of baseball could take a lesson from the competitors here today. That is, if baseball survives."

"Let me see if I can interview some of the players or coaches." Phil Rizzuto climbed down off of the podium, mumbling something about being afraid of heights. "Casey, can you spare a moment?"

Casey left his teammates and sauntered over to meet Mr. Rizzuto. "Sure, Phil. It would be a pleasure to speak to the people of Earth." Casey and Phil shook hands.

Phil: "Are you surprised by the age of the players on the Earth All-Star team?"

Casey: "No, not at all. It was apparent to me that the professional ballplayers were not having much success against us. It was only a matter of time before changes in personnel were made. It is not going to make much difference, however. We are the superior team and we will prove to the universe that no matter who we play, we shall be victorious."

Phil: "Who is going to be your starting pitcher today?"

Casey: "Bob. I expect he will have great success today. He is well prepared."

81

Phil: "One more question. Why the shades?"

Casey: "We wanted to look our best for the cameras."

The interview ended with Casey returning to his bench and Phil walking towards the Earth All-Stars. As he left the interview with Casey, Phil noticed that his hand felt greasy and smelled like honey. "Coach Levy, do you have a moment for our audience?"

"Sure Phil, what's up?" Phil and Coach shook hands, as well.

Phil: "What did you say to your team to prepare them for today's game?"

Coach: "Phil, I've been coaching for many years. I've given hundreds of speeches before, during and after the games. This is the biggest game of all time. The kids know what's at stake. They are motivated and focused. There are billions of people listening to this game. There is nothing I could possibly say to them that they don't already know and feel. Oh, I did tell them one thing. I told them that I love them and I was proud to be their coach."

Phil: "How do you expect to beat the Martians when the major leaguers couldn't defeat them?"

Coach: "The future of baseball and the future of our world rest with our youth. Experience may be the greatest teacher, but preparation is the key to success."

Phil: "Oh, one final question coach. Why the earmuffs?"

Coach: "Didn't the weatherman forecast a cold front for this afternoon?" Coach grinned and returned to his dugout.

"Coach Levy and Casey are now approaching the home plate umpire to present their starting lineups and to discuss the ground rules. Home plate umpire, Ron Kissinger, is pointing out the foul territory behind home and down the first and third base lines. I have been told that there will be no "automatic" home runs today. The umpire has now finished discussing the game rules with the two coaches. Since no one has been designated as the home team, a coin flip will determine who is home and who is away. Earth selects heads. The home plate umpire has flipped the coin. He signals tails. Casey selects his team to be the home team. Coach Levy chooses third base as his dugout. The final game is only minutes away."

"I have just been given the starting lineups for today's game. For the Crestview All-Stars: Shawn will play first base, Ellis will be on second, Glenn at shortstop and Miguel will be at third. In the outfield, Mike will be in left, Stan in center and Patti in right. Pedro, Eric and Carlos will also be in the outfield. Six outfielders. David will be behind the plate. Joni will be pitching. The Crestview All-Star team will be playing 12 players at a time. Apparently, they are taking Casey at his word when he previously announced that Earth could use as many players on the field, at one time, as they want. This game is getting interesting already. For those listening, the last names of the Crestview All-Star players were not announced because they have not been provided by the Coach."

"For the Martians, at first base will be Lou, second base Honus, shortstop Ozzie, and third base Mike. Ted will be in left, Joe in center and Babe in right. The catcher will be Yogi, and pitching today will be Bob. Bob is currently loosening up on the right field foul line, waiting for the signal from the home plate umpire to begin his journey to the pitcher's mound."

"Since there are no sound systems available, the players and coaches have all been asked to stand, with their hats off, while members of each team sing their national anthem."

"The Martians take the field."

CHAPTER THIRTY-SIX

July 16, 2000

Crestview Park

Phil focused his binoculars on Bob, the Martians' starting pitcher. "Bob has completed his warm up in right field and is heading for the mound. In less than five minutes, the final game of the series will begin. No one here on Earth has ever seen Bob pitch. If he is anything like Sandy, the Earth All-Stars will have their work cut out for them. As Bob approaches the infield, he appears a little agitated. There seems to be some kind of insect buzzing all around him. Holy Cow, Bob is now jumping around like he is riding a bucking bronco. He is swatting the insects with his glove. Instead of heading for the mound, he is going back to the dugout."

"What the hell is going on?" Casey asked.

"I don't know," exclaimed Bob. "I started walking across right field and these damn bugs started swarming all over me. It's like I'm attracting them."

Casey took a towel and wiped all of the sunscreen from Bob's arms, legs and neck. He noticed some small bumps around Bob's hands and shoulders. "Does it hurt? Are you able to pitch?"

"I'm fine," Bob said. "Let's get going."

As Bob walked towards the mound, Casey glanced over at Coach Levy. The battle had begun even before the first pitch was thrown.

Rizzuto continued his broadcast. "Bob is allowed nine warm up pitches. Oh my God, the very first pitch hit the backstop on a fly, with Bob falling to the ground."

Casey ran out to the mound to check on his pitcher. "What's going on now?" Casey demanded to know.

"This mound is not like the simulator at all. The hole by the rubber is way too small. I can't fit my foot in there to get any leverage. The hole where my left foot lands is too narrow. I'm losing my balance."

"Try it again," Casey insisted. Casey moved to the side as he watched Bob deliver the next practice pitch. As Bob wound up, his right foot seemed to slip right off the rubber and the pitch one-hopped to Yogi. Casey immediately called Yogi, Sandy and Goose to the mound. "Goose," Casey yelled, "take a towel and rub all the sunscreen off the other players before they get stung, too. Sandy, go up to the Mother Ship and get re-programmed for these measurements."

"It's going to take some time doing it all alone," Sandy explained.

"I know, get going and bring down all of our cleats. I don't trust that Coach Levy at all." Sandy left the field and headed towards the Mother Ship. "Yogi, do you have any suggestions?" Casey inquired.

"Pitch from the set position and forget the full delivery," Yogi instructed. "Shorten up on the stride. It may cut down on the slippage."

"We'll give it a try," Bob stated as he shuffled back to the rubber, "but the program is going to be way off." Bob continued his warm ups with no success. Each pitch found its way to the cage, totally avoiding Yogi's glove.

The home plate umpire officially started the game by yelling "Let's play ball!" Coach Levy instructed the players to be patient. Very patient. He didn't want them swinging at any pitches in the first inning. No matter what.

Rizzutto continued his play-by-play. "Ellis leads off, playing second base. He's five feet, six inches tall, throws right and bats lefty. He has discarded the sunglasses, exchanged the sneakers for a pair of cleats and left the earmuffs back on the bench. He uses an aluminum bat. In fact, from my view, the entire All-Star team has only four bats and all of them are aluminum."

Ellis' bat never left his shoulders. On four consecutive pitches, Ellis walked to first base. The closest pitch was two feet over his head. Bob, using a set delivery and a shortened stride, had no control over his pitches. His fast balls were clocked at 85 mph. He threw no curve balls to Ellis to start the game.

Mike, the left fielder, batted second. At six feet, one inches tall, he was the tallest player on the team. Ellis took a modest lead off first base. Coach manned the third base coach's box while his team was at bat. After every pitch, both Mike and Ellis looked to Coach for any signals. Coach gave them a series of hand signals, ending with his hand rubbing the front of his neck. Bob had still not regained his control. Mike walked on four pitches. Runners were now on first and second with no outs and Joni up next.

The Martian fielders were getting pretty anxious. They had never seen their pitchers throw a ball, let alone eight consecutive ones. Meanwhile, the Crestview bench was ecstatic. The game plan was working to perfection. Coach Levy, however, wondered what Sandy was up to.

Joni was not about to swing away at any of Bob's pitches, whether balls or strikes. She trusted her dad. All the players agreed to follow the game plan to the 't.' Bob was very accommodating. Four more pitches later resulted in the bases being loaded. Casey asked for time, walked to the mound, and called his infield to talk with his pitcher. "Sandy is up on the Mother Ship getting re-programmed," Casey announced. "He should be down in 10 or 15 minutes. Once he is back, I am going to replace Bob with Sandy. I know his arms are tired, but it would look too conspicuous if Bob suddenly regained his form after Sandy returned. Goose is not programmed to go the distance. I'll save him if Sandy gets too tired." Kissinger interrupted the meeting and asked Casey if he was changing pitchers. Casey shook his head no and returned to the bench.

Pedro, David and Miguel, the numbers four through six hitters, all reached base on 12 consecutive balls. Bob was unable to throw strikes. He tried his left arm, right arm, a full wind up, a set delivery, and even a submarine pitch, all with no luck. Three runs scored before one strike had been thrown. Billions of fans were dancing in the streets hoping to be able to play baseball again after today.

By the time Miguel walked in the third run, Sandy had returned from the ship. Casey immediately called time-out and requested a pitching change. With only one day's rest, Sandy returned to the mound after recording two impressive victories in his previous two starts.

It did not take Sandy long to find his new groove. In less than five minutes, he struck out Glenn, Shawn and Patti. At the end of the first half inning, the score was Earth 3 with the Martians coming to bat.

CHAPTER THIRTY-SEVEN

July 16, 2000

Crestview Park

"The Crestview All-Star Team takes the field," Rizzuto announced. "Joni is warming up on the mound, David catching behind the plate. For a 15 year old, Joni has a good, fluid motion reminiscent of Tom Seaver: compact with a burst of energy at the end. The rest of the defense is as follows: Shawn is at first; Ellis is playing a non-traditional second base, almost in shallow centerfield; Glenn, the short stop, is on the edge of the outfield grass; and, Miguel is playing very deep at third. The outfielders: Mike, Stan, Patti, Pedro, Eric and Carlos are positioned three rows deep in left and center. There is no one in right field. Carlos and Eric are playing shallow, Mike and Patti are at normal depth and Stan and Pedro are playing around 450 feet away from home."

"Honus, the second baseman, enters the batter's box against Joni. Dave is in constant motion behind the plate. Joni looks for the sign and delivers the first pitch to Honus: an inside fastball, ball one. Joni's next pitch, another inside fast ball, is rocketed 420 feet to left center field. Pedro circles under the ball for an easy out. In almost any other stadium, it would have been a home run. Honus struts back to the bench, kicking his bat in disgust. One away."

"Joe is up next. Joe decides to bat left handed against Joni. Both the infield and outfield shift again. Now, left field is vacant with all six outfielders covering only center and right. Glenn, the shortstop, is behind second base while the second baseman, Ellis, is on the outfield grass between first and second. Miguel remains at third. Before Joni throws her first pitch, however, Coach Levy calls time, and motions for Carlos with his left arm. Carlos takes over the pitching chores while Joni goes to the outfield. Carlos, a lefty, is the streakier of the two pitchers. He throws hard, often times missing the target. Carlos, completing his abbreviated warm-ups, is now ready to go. Joe remains in his left-handed stance. Carlos glances to Coach, who is standing in front of the All-Star bench. Coach rubs his forehead. All the Martians take note. Joe takes a small step away from home plate towards the edge of the batter's box. Carlos bears down, gets his signal from Dave, and delivers a pitch two inches from Joe's head. Joe hits the deck. Coach calls time and motions for Joni to return to the pitching mound. Carlos returns to the outfield."

"Joni's next two pitches are inside fast balls, both pulled foul down the right field line. Ahead of the count 1 and 2, Miguel joins his teammates on the right side of second. The "Williams" shift is on. Joni continues with her inside pitching, as Joe hits a hard grounder to Ellis for an easy out at first. Two away and here comes Babe."

Carlos and Joni immediately change places again. Coach signals Carlos by rubbing his forehead. Babe sees the signal and digs in a little deeper, his eyes focused on Carlos' left arm. After seeing Carlos' first pitch to Joe, Babe knows what to expect. He got exactly what he expected. The first pitch by Carlos sailed inches over Babe's head, making it to the backstop on a fly. Coach changed pitchers again. Joni continued with her inside pitches. Babe, as his name forecasted, swung for the fences. Unfortunately for him, right field had no fences. His 450-foot towering blast was no more than a "can of corn" to Stan. Through one inning of play; Earth: 3 and Mars: 0.

CHAPTER THIRTY-EIGHT

July 16, 2000

Crestview Park

The second and third innings were scoreless affairs with no runners reaching base. The Crestview All-Stars, leading 3 to 0, did not swing at one pitch from Sandy. Eighteen consecutive strikes were called, resulting in six strike outs. All of Sandy's pitches were fast balls, hitting the inside corners around knee high. Perfect pitches. Whatever problem Bob had in the first with his control, had been remedied by Sandy in the last three innings. If Sandy remained strong, it seemed unlikely that Earth would score any more runs this game. Will a three run lead hold up against this Big Red Machine?

Joni and Carlos continued their mastery over the Martians in innings two and three. Carlos was called on to pitch only once against each batter. It was apparent what his goal was: **FEAR**. Joni did not throw one pitch over the center or outside part of the plate. Every pitch was inside. The Martian hitters refused to "take a walk" or to hit to the opposite field, where there was no one playing. Most balls were hit to the deepest regions of the park, but with six outfielders covering the territory normally occupied by three, no runners reached base.

The most interesting match-up was Joni against Sandy. After Carlos brushed Sandy back with the first pitch, Joni, following Coach's signals, sent a second pitch headed for Sandy's head. Sandy, the only starting pitcher left on Mars' team, couldn't afford to get hurt. Sandy stood on the edge of the batter's box, swinging meekly at Joni's next three offerings. Joni recorded her first strikeout in Inning 3. At the end of three innings, Earth remained in the lead by the score of 3 to 0.

CHAPTER THIRTY-NINE

July 16, 2000

Crestview Park

Coach gathered his team for a quick meeting before the start of the fourth inning.

"Now that you've seen Sandy's pitches, let's get more aggressive. We know that every pitch will be inside and knee high. Sandy is not programmed to throw balls. Every pitch will be the same. Let's get some wood on each pitch. Make Sandy throw as many pitches as possible. If we get on base, look for my signals. The infielders are about to fall asleep, so it is about time to give them a wake-up call."

Rizzuto continued his coverage of the game. "Pedro, the fourth hitter, leads off. He drove in the first run of the game in the first with a walk from Bob. Sandy winds and delivers. Pedro swings and fouls off the pitch into the cage behind the plate. Strike 1."

On Sandy's next delivery, Pedro bunted down the third base line. The ball died in the dirt about 15 feet down the third base line. Mike got a terrible jump on the ball and could not get a throw off to first. Base hit for Pedro. Runner on first, no outs and David was up next.

David, Pedro and Casey stared down at Coach standing in the third base coach's box. Coach's hands were on his hips, interrupted by an occasional hand clap. He did, however, wipe his feet in the dirt. Casey scratched his head as David readied himself for the next pitch from Sandy. Sandy's first pitch, inside and knee high, was bunted down the third base line, almost in the exact same spot as Pedro's. Mike, who was playing even with the bag, made a throw to first, but the umpire called David safe. Runners on first and second, no outs.

Casey called time-out and met with his pitcher and infielders. "Sandy," Casey demanded, "can't you throw to a different spot than inside and knee high?"

"That's all I was able to program," Sandy proclaimed, "unless I disconnect the chip. But if I do that, there is no way of knowing where the pitches may go."

"No, no, no. Don't do that," quipped Casey. "We can't afford any more runs." Casey turned his attention to the infielders. "Look, these kids can't hit. Play close. Real close. If I have to, I'll bring in the outfield, as well." Casey left the mound less confident that his team was prepared to take control of this game.

Miguel, the sixth hitter, stepped up to the plate. While Casey had met with his team, Coach and Miguel had met with David and Pedro to review signals. Sandy's first two pitches were strikes. Miguel let both of them go without a swing. Miguel looked down at Coach, who slowly tipped his hat towards the batter. Miguel acknowledged the sign. He entered the batter's box, awaiting Sandy's delivery. David and Miguel took leads as Sandy threw home. Miguel chopped the ball into the ground, bouncing it 20 feet into the air. There was no play at any base. The bases were loaded, no outs, and Glenn, the shortstop, the seventh hitter, due up next. This was the second time that Glenn had faced Sandy. In the first, Glenn had struck out on three pitches. He promised himself, this time, the outcome would be different.

Casey had enough. He stood on the bench, waving a towel to the attention of the outfielders. Casey directed them to play shallow. Real shallow. By the time the shift was finished, all nine fielders were surrounding the infield. The outfield was vacant.

Coach patted his head as Glenn readied himself at the plate. Sandy's pitch was hit in the air towards right center field. All three outfielders converged on the fly: Ted from deep short, Joe from shallow center and Babe from deep second. The trio was unable to catch the routine fly. The runners were off and flying. As the ball hit the ground, it landed on the "cat's tail" and ricocheted towards the right field line. Babe was nearest the ball when the bees started to attack. He tried in vain to get the ball, but it rolled to a stop a few feet away from the nest. Babe kicked the ball with his foot to Joe, who was able to make a throw home. Glenn slid under Yogi's tag as four more runs crossed the plate. A grand slam.

Casey had no one to blame but himself. The next three batters, after fouling off numerous pitchers, all grounded to second. The score at the end of 3½ innings: Earth 7 and Mars 0.

CHAPTER FORTY

July 16, 2000

Crestview Park

Casey was fit to be tied. His mighty Martians were losing by a score of 7 to 0 to a bunch of Little Leaguers. Casey instructed his team to wait for good pitches, not to go "downtown" on every swing, to go to the opposite field and to bunt on occasion. He reminded his fellow Martians that Carlos had not thrown one strike yet and they should not be intimidated by his inside pitching. Finally, he told his team that Sandy probably had three more innings left to pitch and then Goose was going to pitch the eighth and ninth innings.

The umpire motioned for Honus to enter the batter's box. Joni's first pitch, inside and high, was bunted down the third base line. The bunt, like David's and Pedro's earlier that inning, died in the dirt, 10 feet down the third base line. But as Honus attempted to move quickly out of the box, his feet sunk deeper and deeper into the dirt. Honus' poor start gave David the time to pounce on the ball and throw him out at first base. One out. Joni had still not allowed a runner on base.

With the shift in place, Joni next faced Joe, batting lefty. She continued with her barrage of inside pitches, this time running the count to three and two. Making her first bad pitch of the day, Joe drilled the payoff pitch to left, an area vacated by the shift. With the left field ground hardened by the lack of rain, the ball skidded into no-man's land for a home run. The Earth's lead was cut to 7-1. No one on the Crestview All-Stars was concerned, especially after Joni got Babe to fly deep to center and Ted to ground to first. At the end of the fourth, the score was Earth 7 and Mars 1.

CHAPTER FORTY-ONE

July 16, 2000

Crestview Park

Coach instructed his players to continue to wear Sandy down. The sooner he was gone, the greater Earth's chances of success. Over the course of the next three innings, Sandy threw 60 pitches with no less than five pitches thrown to any one hitter. The All-Stars were implementing their game plan to perfection. Well, almost.

With the Martians down by six runs with only three innings to play, Casey turned on the heat. He got "in the face" with every one of his players, making them remember why they were there, and the consequences to each and every one of them if Mars lost. He finally convinced them that going for the home run was not the path to success, but smart baseball would be the key to victory. The Martians responded with new vitality. Did the All-Stars have enough energy left to stop the attack?

With the shift in place, Honus led off the seventh inning with an opposite field hit between first and second. The Martians had never had their lead runner on base before. Carlos came in to face Joe. After "brushing" Joe back, Carlos returned to the outfield. The Carlos/Joni strategy was becoming old hat. Joe singled through the hole in left, advancing Honus to second. Babe, putting his home run swing away, bunted down the third base line. Everyone was caught off-guard. Bases were loaded with no one out.

Coach Levy called time and walked to the mound to confer with Joni and David. "How's your arm?" Coach asked Joni.

"I feel fine. We need to change strategy, Dad. They are finding the openings in our defense."

"I know. I'm going to even out the infield and place one fielder in left or right, depending on which side of the plate they bat. We can't afford not to play deep, especially if they keep hitting the long ball," Coach replied.

"Can I move the ball around the plate more?" Joni asked.

"Okay, then give them your whole arsenal. Dave, make sure the players are positioned correctly."

"Okay, Coach," Dave responded.

"Oh, Dave, make some noise back there," Coach stated. Coach winked at Dave as he walked off the mound. Before returning to the bench, Coach repositioned his players: the "shift" of the infield was eliminated and Mike was placed back in left field. The game plan was back to square one.

Despite the bases being full of Martians, Joni gripped the ball with renewed confidence. She decided to pull out her entire bag of tricks. Ted, batting cleanup, was ready. All day long, Joni's pitches had been inside. Ted, despite his long arms, was not prepared for Joni's first pitch on the outside corner. Strike one. Joni's next pitch was a sight to behold. *A la* Steve Hamilton, Joni threw her infamous "folly floater," a high-arcing rainbow that would have been more at home on the softball field. Ted couldn't believe what he saw. All of what Casey had "lectured" had gone in one ear and out the same. Ted's eye lit up. He swung as hard as he could, topping the ball to first base. Shawn cleanly fielded the grounder, raced to the bag for the first out and threw home to Dave. Having removed the force at home, Dave needed to tag Honus for the out. As Dave received Shawn's throw home, two worlds collided. Dave miraculously held onto the ball as the umpire raised his right hand and "punched out" Honus. Casey rushed to the plate to argue the call. He stomped, yelled, spit and shouted without success. Casey's hat, like his team, was now a little frayed. The only thing he had managed to do was to create a dust bowl around home plate.

Meanwhile, David lay motionless on top of home plate. Coach, Joni and the rest of the team rushed to his aid. Paramedics and trainers rushed from the stands. It took several minutes before David was able to regain consciousness. He was placed on a stretcher and taken to a nearby hospital. As he was being loaded into the ambulance, David reached his hand out to grab Coach's arm. David whispered, "kick their butts."

Coach nodded and said, "consider it done."

Joni had been shaken by the collision at home. Time was called to allow Eric to replace Dave as the catcher. The outfield now consisted of five fielders: one in left, two in center and two in right. Joni's mind was not focused as she delivered her first pitch to Lou. Batting left-handed, Lou drilled one into the gap in left-center. Patti got a good jump on the ball, but forgot about the drainage ditch. As she was about 10 feet from the ball, Patti's spikes caught in the ditch. She crumpled to the ground as if shot, grabbing her right ankle. With Patti unable to make the catch, the ball rolled to Yaz field, allowing all three runners to score.

The Crestview All-Stars were suddenly disheartened, demoralized and dejected. Despite having a three run lead, and needing only seven more outs for victory, the momentum was clearly with the Martians. By looking at the two benches, one could not tell which team was winning.

After Patti left the field in the ambulance, the game resumed. Joni remained on the mound. The outfield now consisted of four players. The players were positioned in an "umbrella" formation, positioned alongside the foul lines and the left and right field "alleyways." All players were positioned deep, willing to sacrifice a single or double.

Joni had a long talk with her dad during the 30-minute game delay. He told her to forget about David and Patti, at least for now, and concentrate on her pitching. David and Patti's injuries would heal, he said, but a loss today would remain a wound for generations to come. The home field advantage had served its purpose; now it was time for inner determination and willpower to take hold.

Regardless of the pep talk, Joni had never faced such a formidable opponent, especially under these conditions. All of her thoughts went beyond the hitters facing her – whether David and Patti were okay, whether baseball would ever be played again, whether she would be held responsible for the Martians' victory... her thoughts were abruptly interrupted by the cry of "Play ball" from the home plate umpire.

All Joni needed was one more out to end the seventh. Yogi was the next batter. It didn't take long to realize that Joni was still not herself. On the very first pitch, Yogi lined a single to right field. Since Pedro was playing so deep, Yogi made it to second without even a slide. Ozzie then bunted down the third base line, catching Miguel taking 40 winks. Runners on first and third, two outs, and Mike, the tying run, was up next. Mike was the number-eight hitter. Goose, who was to start pitching in the top of the eighth, was on deck. After a brief meeting on the mound with Coach, Eric and Joni, it was decided to walk Mike and pitch to Goose.

Casey called Goose back to the bench to remind him of the strategy: don't go for the home run, don't be a hero, just make contact. Casey could just as well have been on Mars, for Goose didn't hear one word he said. All Goose could visualize was the celebration for him on Mars as the hero who hit the grand slam to beat Earth 8 to 7.

Joni stood on the pitcher's mound scanning the field that was her "home." She made eye contact with every one of her teammates. Each one nodded their heads, reassuring Joni, visually and emotionally, that they were behind her 100%. Joni tipped her cap to her teammates and turned to face Goose. There was no way, Joni told herself, that Goose was going to beat her. She visualized each pitch and the outcome she expected.

Three pitches later, her teammates were running off the field, heading for their bench. Goose was kicking dirt all the way back to Mars. His dream of glory quickly faded in the summer heat. Now, he had to face Casey, his worst nightmare. After 7 innings, Earth 7-Mars 4.

Only six outs remained between happiness and doom. The Crestview All-Stars were drained and under-staffed, with two of their teammates hospitalized. The weight of the world seemed too heavy for these teenagers to bear. The Martians, on the other hand, were cowering under Casey's dark shadow. As Casey paced the sidelines in front of his bench, steam was literally coming out of his head. Little did the Martians know that Casey was personally blaming himself for his team's situation. He had been out-coached and outsmarted by an unknown Earthling who had never played professional sports – of any kind. Casey had made wrong coaching decisions by pulling the outfield in too close in the fourth and by allowing Goose to hit for Sandy. Most of all, he had been "out-scouted." For the first time, an opposing coach knew more about his team than he knew about theirs.

Casey would not allow Mars to be defeated, even if he had to personally become involved in the outcome.

The eighth inning produced minimal excitement. Nothing could compare to the bizarre occurrences of the seventh. Goose, trying to make amends for his batting fiasco, was un-hittable. The All-Stars went down in order in both the eighth and ninth innings. Goose desperately wanted one more chance at the plate.

Joni regained her composure in the bottom of the eighth. Besides giving up long foul balls, Joni retired Honus, Joe and Babe in order. The stage was set for one final showdown.

CHAPTER FORTY-TWO

The Martians were down by three,
with but an inning left to play,
their hopes were fading fast,
to conquer Earth this day.

Joni was throwing heat,
from her favorite pitcher's mound,
Fly balls were caught for outs,
or hit weakly into the ground.

As the world listened on,
To Rizzuto's blow-by-blow,
Ted and Lou flied out,
only one more out to go.

But Yogi, Ozzie and Mike
were determined not to be
the final Martian to make an out,
and face the anger of Casey.

All three walked to first,
with Joni needing a rest,
Goose was waiting on deck,
clearly not the Martian's best.

Rizzuto's voice began to crackle,
It must have been fate,
For Goose returned to the bench,
as Casey strode to the plate.

Coach Levy called time,
to talk with his ace.
It was time for a change,
to pick up the pace.

Carlos, the flamethrower,
was ready to burn.
Casey grabbed his lumber,
awaiting his turn.

The stage was set
between young and old,
a battle for the ages,
the winner getting the gold.

Carlos' first pitch
Blazed like the sun.
Casey swung his mighty bat,
The umpire shouted, "strike one."

Gary H. Goldberg

Carlos reared back
and threw some more smoke.
Casey got all of it,
a truly mighty poke.

The ball traveled far
as Earth caught its breath.
If it stayed fair,
it would surely mean death...

For baseball was truly
a game of inches this day,
the blast just went foul,
it was barely out of play.

Casey was ready
for one more dart,
Carlos threw a change,
he really had heart.

Casey swung from his toes,
trying to kill that damn ball,
"Strike three," shouted the ump,
Baseball was back for all.

The Crestview *Monitor*
July 17, 2000

CHAPTER FORTY-THREE

<u>Hall of Fame Induction Weekend</u>

<u>August, 2000</u>

The Hall of Fame induction ceremonies were extra special this year. A new exhibit was displayed, commemorating Earth's success in the first, and hopefully last, intergalactic series. "Baseball Lives" depicted video of the first two games of the Series, the entire radio broadcast of the final game against the Crestview All-Stars, and memorabilia: a Martian hat and glove, an autographed baseball from the Crestview All-Stars, Patti's cast from her broken ankle and a still photograph of the site of the final game: Crestview Park.

Two additional items were placed in a special glass enclosure. The first was the letter sent to the Commissioner from Coach Levy which persuaded the Commissioner to allow the Crestview All-Stars to play the Martians.

Dear Commissioner Johnson:

My name is George Levy. I coach a Babe Ruth League All-Star Team from Crestview, Massachusetts. I have discovered the secret to Mars' baseball prowess.

Mars has been monitoring Earth for years. They apparently know everything about us. In order for Earth to win, we must reclaim the element of surprise. Our professional ballplayers are well known to the Martians. The Martians must have a "record" on each and every ballplayer. In order for Sandy to be so successful, he must know the absolute best place to pitch each one of our hitters. For Sandy to implement this game plan, he also must know the exact dimensions of the mound, texture of the dirt, the wind speed, etc. Even with that knowledge, Sandy must execute flawlessly. No person on Earth could throw 81 perfect pitches without a slight deviation at times. That must mean that Sandy's pitches are computerized or programmed in advance. You may recall he did not throw one ball. I believe that their pitchers are incapable of throwing balls due to their programming. If we were able to surprise them by hiding the identity of their opposition and the playing field itself, their level of preparation would be deficient. If the pitching is not programmed in advance, we will be able to hit them effectively.

As to their hitting abilities, there is a field that our All-Stars play on that may give us a slight advantage. The Crestview All-Stars welcome the opportunity to represent our world in the final game against the Martians. Their age and size will further heighten the element of surprise.

Additionally, it is the children who would be most affected by the loss of baseball in the future. They deserve the opportunity to play for the future of baseball. Time is of the essence. You can reach me at 508-555-2255. Please be careful. All of our calls may be monitored.

Very truly yours,

George Levy

Adjacent to the letter was the final item in the now-famous collection: a Samuel Adams beer bottle.

The End

Printed in the United States
202825BV00001B/58-105/A

9 781418 418830